# Daily Blessings
## for My
# Husband

Daily Blessings for My Husband
ISBN 1-59027-037-1

Copyright © 2002 by GRQ Ink, Inc.
1948 Green Hills Boulevard
Franklin, Tennessee 37067

Published by Popular Publishing Company
3 Park Avenue
New York, New York 10016

Developed by GRQ Ink, Inc.
Manuscript written by Melody Carlson
Cover and text design by Richmond & Williams
Composition by Educational Publishing Concepts, Inc.

# Daily Blessings
## for My
# Husband

THE
## POPULAR
GROUP

New York, New York

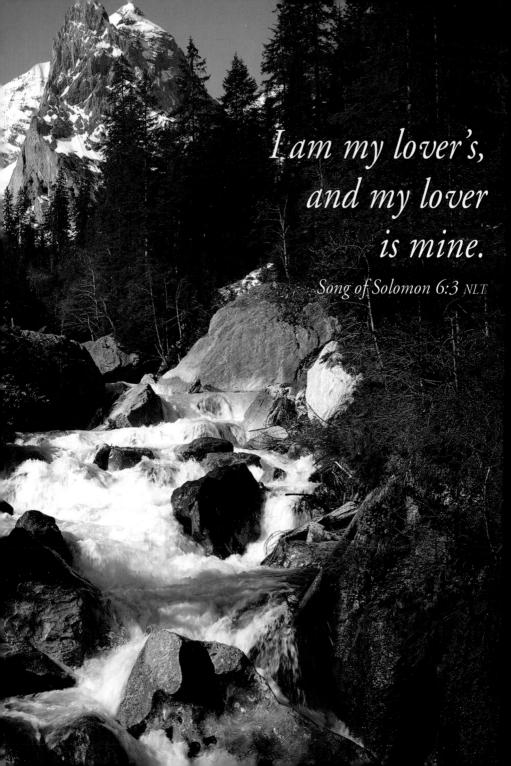

*I am my lover's,
and my lover
is mine.*

*Song of Solomon 6:3* NLT

And the Lord God said, "It is not good that man should be alone; I will make him a helper comparable to him."

GENESIS 2:18 NKJV

*My Dear Husband,*

*Our love is one of life's greatest blessings.*

*I want you to know how much you mean to me—how much I love you. And I want to assure you that I believe in our marriage. I long for the two of us to grow closer and more in love than ever before.*

*But sometimes it's difficult to put such heartfelt feelings into words.*

*And so, I hope this little book will communicate my deepest thoughts and desires for you and for our relationship. And as you read these simple words each day, I hope that you will receive them as a gift from my heart to yours.*

*Because I love you,*

*Your Wife*

# I Choose to Love You

*Dear friends, let us love one another, for love comes from God.
Everyone who loves has been born of God and knows God.*

1 JOHN 4:7 NIV

*My Dear Husband,*

*I bless you with my heartfelt love. I want you to know that I am committed to love you—fully and completely—today and every day for the rest of our lives. Do you remember the zealous time of youth when we believed our love for each other would always flow with heat and fervent passion like a brightly burning flame? Now, of course, we understand that the tension of daily living can put a damper on our passion at times.*

*Some marriages fall apart when the flame of passion grows dim, but my love for you will remain strong when the flame is burning fiercely and also when it flickers. For, you see, I have chosen to love you—for a lifetime. I rejoice in the commitment I have made to you. It is written upon the pages of my heart.*

---

*Dear God, we come before You this day, reaffirming our love for one another and for You. Continue to touch our marriage with Your hand of blessing, we pray. Amen.*

# Made for Each Other

**For You formed my inward parts;**
**You covered me in my mother's womb.**

PSALM 139:13 NKJV

~∞~

My Dear Husband,

You are so very right for me. God made you especially for me—I know it! Each day, I see how perfectly our strengths and weaknesses are being woven together to create a beautiful tapestry. I am so much stronger, so much more courageous, so much more virtuous, so much more fulfilled because you are in my life. Together, we can accomplish anything God asks of us. With His hand of blessing upon our heads, we cannot be defeated.

Do you remember that once we allowed our differences to draw us apart? We think so differently, see issues from differing perspectives, respond differently to the things that happen around us. But we have learned that our differences are the very qualities that give our marriage strength and color and vibrancy. Completing our tapestry will take a lifetime. But as we work together, we will continue to weave a masterpiece.

―――――― ~∞~ ――――――

Dear God, we thank You wholeheartedly for making us just the way we are. And we pray that we will both be transformed into all that You would have us become. Amen.

# My Promise to You

**A man must leave his father and mother when he marries, so
that he can be perfectly joined to his wife,
and the two shall be one.**

EPHESIANS 5:31 TLB

*My Dear Husband,*

*I bless you for keeping your promise. Do you remember the day we stood
before God and vowed to love and honor each other for as long as we both
should live? It was an emotional day, a memorable day, overflowing with
roses and promises. It was a day filled with bright expectations and sincere
hopes and dreams. It was a day I will always hold close and remember
fondly.*

*Do you recall how I trembled as I looked into your eyes and repeated
my vows? I remember the warm security of your embrace and the heat of
your kiss. And although time has passed and the roses have faded, my
promise to you remains the same. I shall love you as long as I have breath.*

---

*Dear God, help us to reaffirm our promise to love and cherish one
another on a daily basis. Help us to remember that our marriage vows were
made not only to each other, but also to You. Help us to keep them. Amen.*

# The First Time I Saw You

*My beloved is white and ruddy,*
*Chief among ten thousand.*
*His head is like the finest gold;*
*His locks are wavy.*

SONG OF SOLOMON 5:10-11 NKJV

ᘒ

My Dear Husband,

You will always be my hero. I remember that unforgettable moment when I first saw you as the person with whom I wanted to spend the rest of my life. In that moment, you became my handsome knight in shining armor—the hero who would slay a fiery dragon to rescue me. And that's when I gave you my heart. I knew we would live happily ever after.

Our marriage has not been the perfect fairy tale we imagined, but you are still my prince. I still feel a glow of excitement and pride when you walk into the room. You will always be my hero, my dragon slayer. I bless the day I placed my hand in yours.

Dear God, help us to always remember how we felt when our love was new. And help us to renew our love day by day, in good times and bad, in the storms and in the sunshine. Amen.

# Hidden Places in Our Hearts

*Would not God find this out?*
*For He knows the secrets of the heart.*

PSALM 44:21 NAS

*M*y Dear Husband,

*I bless you for your hidden depths. Sometimes I watch you when you're unaware that I am looking. And I wonder—what's going on inside that man I love so much? What is he thinking; what is he feeling? For, although we are close, I realize that there are still hidden places in your heart (just as there are in mine)—places where I cannot yet go.*

*Perhaps those places are uncharted territories for you and, until now, unfathomable to you as well. Perhaps you are only now exploring them yourself. When you are ready, I am anxious to hear of your adventures there. And I long to share some findings of my own, from places within my own heart. And in time, with love and trust and patience, perhaps our two hearts can truly become one.*

---

*D*ear God, *show us the secrets hidden in the depths of our own hearts. And help us to create a strong foundation of mutual trust that will allow us to invite each other in. Amen.*

# What Were You Like?

**When I was a child, I spoke as a child, I understood as a child, I thought as a child; but when I became a man, I put away childish things.**

1 CORINTHIANS 13:11 NKJV

*My* Dear Husband,

I love the little boy in you. I try to imagine you as a small child running barefoot in the grass, playing army soldiers, climbing a big cherry tree, or putting a frog in your pocket. Such thoughts make me smile. I look at your childhood photos and imagine all sorts of things about the charming little boy there. How I wish I had known the child that you were. I think that I would have liked him very much!

I can imagine myself sitting enthralled, listening as you spin your greatest dreams and share your worst fears. I know I would be delighted to find out the little things—like how you felt about asparagus and whether you were in love with your teenaged babysitter. I would have loved you then, in my own childish way, just as I love you now.

---

*Dear* God, I realize how many of the things we experienced in childhood make us who we are today. Help us to learn more about the children that we were so that we can better appreciate the adults we are now.

# Kindred Spirits

**That their hearts may be encouraged, being knit together in love, and attaining to all riches of the full assurance of understanding, to the knowledge of the mystery of God, both of the Father and of Christ.**

COLOSSIANS 2:2 NKJV

*My* Dear Husband,

*I bless you for being my other half. I want to be your soul mate—the person you turn to when you need someone to listen—the one you trust with the deepest secrets of your heart. Do you think we can do that for each other? It's a tall order, but with time and God's help, I think we can do it.*

*I truly believe that when two people come together before God as husband and wife, He opens their hearts to one another in a miraculous way. He makes it possible for them to become kindred spirits. And despite our many differences, I think we fit together beautifully; and our strengths and weaknesses complement one another.*

---

*Dear God, only You are able to knit our hearts together and make us one in Your love. We pray that You will teach us to be willing—and that you will increase our love for one another. Amen.*

# Even When We Don't Agree

**Blessed are the peacemakers,
for they will be called children of God.**

MATTHEW 5:9 NRSV

*My Dear Husband,*

*I love that our hearts can agree. Isn't it nice that we don't always have to agree on every single thing? We each have a mind of our own—and I think that makes life vastly more interesting. Or, as one person wisely said, "If we always agreed on everything, then one of us would be unnecessary." What an insight!*

*So, my love, let's agree to disagree. But let's do it peacefully. Let's welcome those lively discussions, enjoy a good debate, and practice some active listening. But let's take care not to become offensive or defensive, and let's not put each other down when we find ourselves on differing sides of an issue. Let's try hard to see the other point of view. For after all, two heads really are better than one.*

*Dear God, teach us to celebrate our differences and respect our opposing opinions. Help us to practice love and patience and tolerance, always appreciating the strength we find in varying perspectives. Amen.*

# What Are You Thinking?

*You know when I sit down and when I rise up;*
*you discern my thoughts from far away.*

PSALM 139:2 NRSV

⌒⌒⌒

*My Dear Husband,*

*I want to know your mind. I've noticed that you seem quiet when you come home some days. You go silently about your business and keep to yourself. Before long, I begin to feel left out and wonder if I've done something wrong. I often worry that something has gone wrong for you during the day or that you are carrying a burden or that you are struggling with a decision I don't know about.*

*I want you to know that I am here to listen, to offer a warm hug or a shoulder to cry on, if that is what you need. I am also willing to pray quietly for you and give you the space you need to think things through and process your thoughts. Whatever the case, you can count on me. I am on your side always, my love.*

⌒⌒⌒

*Dear God, help us to respect the fact that people sometimes need space to think and process their thoughts. Give us the patience we need to provide that for each other. Amen.*

# It's Hard to Wait

*For I am waiting for you, O Lord my God.*
*Come and protect me.*

PSALM 38:15 TLB

*My Dear Husband,*

*I bless you for your own unique pace. I know I'm pretty impatient at times. Like a child waiting for Christmas, I get all wrought up waiting for things to happen. I want our marriage to be better, our home to be prettier, our lives to be more fulfilling. And although I know my expectations are for positive things, I don't always want to wait for God's timing. I tend to want to anticipate and hurry along. That can make me difficult to live with sometimes.*

*Please understand, my love. I'm learning to accept that God's timing isn't always my timing. I want to trust Him more completely for what I think I need right now. I pray that soon you will be pleased with the patience God is working in my life.*

---

*Dear God, teach us to appreciate that You have our lives and our days in Your hands. Remind us that Your timing is always perfect. Help us to help each other as we wait on You. Amen.*

# A Really Good Date

*David said to Abigail, "Blessed be the LORD, the God of Israel,
who sent you to meet me today!"*

1 SAMUEL 25:32 NRSV

*My Dear Husband,*

*I love how our love heats up. Do you wonder like I do how to stir up passion and romance in our relationship? Perhaps we should go out on a date periodically. Just you and me. No children; no friends. Just the two of us alone together. Whether we walk together on the beach with the wind blowing through our hair or sit in a quiet, candlelit restaurant, let's make it a special time—a time for celebrating our love for each other. It really doesn't matter so much what we do but that we do it. I long to keep alive the wonder of our love and to make sure we kindle it gently with our continuing affections.*

*I warn you, I plan to look deeply into your eyes and I may reach for your hand. But I hope you'll be looking into my eyes and reaching for my hand as well. We have a lot of love to share!*

*Dear God, give us real romance—the kind where we simply lose ourselves in each other. And, Lord, help us to remember to thank You for planting the seed of love in our hearts. Amen.*

# We Need Trust

**Like the coolness of snow at harvest time is a trustworthy
messenger to those who send him;
he refreshes the spirit of his masters.**

PROVERBS 25:13 NIV

My Dear Husband,

I trust you with my heart. What is more essential to a healthy friendship
than trust? In fact, it is the most basic element of any good relationship.
And for our marriage to be all it can possibly be, we must learn to trust
each other—implicitly, no matter what, when, or where. But I know that
kind of trust doesn't happen overnight. It takes time and circumstances and
just plain life to build a solid foundation of trust. And yet, we are building
it—daily.

Each day that we remain loyal and loving to each other, we place a new
stone of trust into our foundation. Let's partner together to build a strong
foundation for trust.

---

Dear God, we need Your divine help to build a solid marriage. And we
need You to help us to become dependable and faithful partners. We need You
to teach us how to trust each other. Amen.

# Let's Fellowship

*But if we live in the light, as God is in the light, we can share fellowship with each other. Then the blood of Jesus, God's Son, cleanses us from every sin.*

1 JOHN 1:7 NCV

൞൞

*M*y Dear Husband,

*I love seeing you with others. I love spending time with you and I hope you love spending time with me. But, we both know that we also need other people in our lives. We each need to develop friendships, and if we can enjoy the company of others, as a couple, that's even better. Opening our lives to others allows us to give and receive encouragement and insights. And we especially need people in our lives who believe as we do—people who want to love and share and worship our God with us.*

*So, let's make a plan (or maybe just recommit to one) that we will spend time with others. Let's enjoy the fellowship God has graciously provided for us. And let's learn together as a group how to follow after God with our whole hearts.*

൞൞

*D*ear God, show us where and when we need to spend times in fellowship. And help us to get in the habit of going and sharing—and building relationships with others. Amen.

# When the Workday Is Done

*Let us do our best to go into that place of rest, too,
being careful not to disobey God . . .
thus failing to get in.*

HEBREWS 4:11 TLB

༄༅༅

My Dear Husband,

I love when we can relax together. Oh, how I look forward to seeing your face when we come back together after a long and busy day. And I suppose I set myself up with all sorts of expectations. Perhaps I'm discouraged and hoping you'll lift my spirits. Or maybe I feel happy and want to celebrate. But what I often forget is that your day may have been the opposite of mine.

And sometimes we're just out of sync, or maybe we've both had a rotten day, and we both feel needy and unable to give. Occasionally emotions rise too quickly to the surface, and we say things we don't really mean. So, let's plan for these moments, considering one another and how we can make our reunion more pleasant.

———————— ༄༅༅ ————————

Dear God, as we look forward to coming back together at the end of the day, help us to seek out new ways to listen and encourage each other. Amen.

# The Need to Nurture

*If one member suffers, all suffer together with it;*
*if one member is honored,*
*all rejoice together with it.*

1 CORINTHIANS 12:26 NRSV

*My Dear Husband,*

I bless you for being here for me. I like taking care of things, keeping life running smoothly and everyone happy. Perhaps it's just part of my makeup—the need to nurture. And nurturing is good. But sometimes I need to let you nurture me. You may not know this, but you have the innate ability to minister to me and make me feel special like no one else in my life can.

So let's take care of each other. Each day, I will look for ways to ease your stress, encourage your heart, and help you grow stronger in your sense of confidence and well-being. And I will receive with joy the ways in which you nurture me.

---

*Dear God, show us ways to nurture and build each other up. Teach us to be sensitive to each other's needs. And help us to appreciate the love and caring You've placed in our hearts for each other. Amen.*

# When We Fight

*"In your anger do not sin": Do not let the sun go down while you are still angry, and do not give the devil a foothold.*

EPHESIANS 4:26-27 NIV

*My Dear Husband,*

*I love it when we make up. Most people will agree that fighting is a natural part of marriage—no couple agrees on everything all the time (or if they do, they must be boring!). I don't ever want to fight with you, but I know there will be times when my human nature will get the best of me. Before that happens, I want to make you these promises:*

*\* I will be careful not to call you names.*

*\* I will refuse to dredge up old offenses.*

*\* I won't use phrases like "you always" and "you never."*

*\* I will listen to what you have to say with an open mind.*

*\* I will never criticize you to others.*

*\* I will do my best to never go to bed angry.*

---

*Dear God, teach us to live peaceably together, but if we need to clear the air, help us to do it in a healthy and wholesome way. And may our marriage be stronger for it. Amen.*

# I Need to Be Heard

*Don't just pretend that you love others.*
*Really love them. Hate what is wrong.*
*Stand on the side of the good.*

ROMANS 12:9 NLT

*My Dear Husband,*

*I bless you for listening. Sometimes you must feel that I'm not really listening to you. Perhaps I'm distracted by the TV, involved with projects around the house, or just caught up in my own private thoughts. If this should happen, please don't think that I don't care about you or what you have to say. To me, your words are always important. I look to you for loving feedback.*

*Just remember that I'm human and sometimes I forget that nothing is more important than our relationship with each other and with God. I hope that you will gently remind me when I'm set on hyper speed and not paying attention to the more important things around me.*

---

*Dear God, help us to be sensitive to each other and never let the superficial cares and responsibilities of everyday life keep us from loving and caring for each other. Amen.*

# I Have a Dream

*We were like those who dream.*
*Then our mouth was filled with laughter,*
*And our tongue with singing . . .*
*"The Lord has done great things."*

PSALM 126:1-2 NKJV

*My Dear Husband,*

*I love to share your dreams. Deep within each of us is a dream—maybe it's from childhood, maybe it's from adolescence, or maybe it is brand-new this very morning. It could be silly and frivolous, or serious and intense. Or perhaps it's spiritual and rather difficult to understand. But do you know what my dreams are made of? Do you know what my secret desires might be?*

*To really know a person, you need to know their dreams, their desires. There's so much more to us than what we see. And love can slowly bring new things to the surface—just like peeling layer after layer off of an onion, so it can be with us.*

*Dear God, teach us to dream. Help us to share our dreams with each other. Show us how to dream together. Amen.*

# Let's Light a Candle

**My beloved said to me, "Rise up, my love, my fair one, and come away."**

SONG OF SOLOMON 2:10 TLB

*My Dear Husband,*

*I love it when we're together. Let's celebrate romance. Let's plan for a quiet evening at home with fresh flowers, soft music—and let's light some candles. There is something so deeply romantic about the soft, golden glow of candlelight—the way it flickers and casts its delicate light across your skin, the delicious smell of fragrant melting wax, and the warmth of its luminescence as it gently lights the room. The soft scents of musk and rose and jasmine will enhance the expression of our love.*

*Let's take time to relax and soak in the soft romantic light. Let's talk quietly and intimately, and let's enjoy each other's company. I want to look deeply into your eyes and see the flame of candlelight reflected there—and see the light of love.*

*Dear God, thank You for the gift of romantic love. Life seems so much sweeter when the candlelight is shared by two. Amen.*

# Healing Our Past

The LORD is close to the brokenhearted, and he saves those
whose spirits have been crushed. People who do what is right
may have many problems, but the LORD will solve them all.

PSALM 34:18 NCV

*My Dear Husband,*

*I love how we can "move on" together. When we entered into our
marriage, we both brought along some extra baggage. We were aware of
some things and other things we'd forgotten or thought we'd left behind. But
as the years pass, old memories resurface, coming out when we least expect
them. We soon realize that many wounds from childhood and youth still
remain with us. And sometimes they impair our adulthood.*

*So, let's tell each other about the old hurts that never seem to go
completely away. Let's acknowledge them and earnestly pray for each other.
And with this new awareness our compassion and understanding for each
other will expand—and the healing will begin.*

*Dear God, help us recognize and acknowledge the old hurts that have
wounded us. Help us to bring them to You, to pray for each other, and to
expect Your healing touch. Amen.*

# The Others in Our Lives

*A man should leave his father and mother, and be forever
united to his wife. The two shall become one—no longer two,
but one!*

MATTHEW 19:5-6 TLB

*My Dear Husband,*

*I love seeing you reach out to others. Sometimes I think if you and I
lived together, all by ourselves, off on a deserted, tropical island
somewhere—I think then we could be perfectly happy. Well, at least for a
couple of weeks anyway. But there's no getting away from all the other
people in our lives; they both bless our lives and complicate them.*

*Therefore, I want you to know that I will always value your opinion
and respect your wishes more than anyone else's. I will put you above my
family, my friends, my career, my own needs and desires. I will put you
first. In my heart, only God will be higher. I count it an honor to be your
wife.*

*Dear God, help us to place our relationship above all other earthly
ones. And teach us how to maintain good priorities: putting You first in all
things, our marriage second, and everyone else after that. Amen.*

# How You Can Help Me

*Yes indeed, it is good when you truly obey our Lord's command, "You must love and help your neighbors just as much as you love and take care of yourself."*

JAMES 2:8 TLB

*My Dear Husband,*

*I bless you for your strength. I know how I might sometimes come across as fairly self sufficient and capable. I'm always trying to keep things under control and everyone on track. But underneath that veneer of togetherness, I am sometimes falling completely apart inside. I'm grateful that God gave me someone like you to lean on—someone who is strong and trustworthy and kind.*

*When you jump in to help me, suddenly any task seems doable. I feel immediate relief when your strength backs my efforts, when your strength doubles mine. It's fun working with you—and it's true that many hands make light work. And just think of what fun we can have once we're done!*

*Dear God, teach us how to work together. Help us to help each other. Show us some new ways to establish a team spirit when it comes to getting the job done. Amen.*

# What Makes You Tick?

*I will be glad and rejoice in your love,
for you saw my affliction
and knew the anguish of my soul.*

PSALM 31:7 NIV

*My Dear Husband,*

*I love learning more about you. Thank goodness, we're so vastly different. Have you noticed how one thing totally sets me off, but hardly fazes you? Another situation pushes all your buttons and I could care less. Yes, what a blessing we have such varying temperaments.*

*Just the same, I sometimes wonder what makes you do the things you do. Is it genetics? A predisposition? Did you have a bad day? A good day? And why do some things tick you off? And the reason I want to know is so I can help you. Perhaps I'll see something before you do. Perhaps I can send a gentle warning. Or maybe I can just pray. So, tell me, what makes you tick?*

---

*Dear God, teach us how to be a blessing to each other, a leveling influence. Help us to learn to depend on each other to keep our perspectives well balanced. Amen.*

# An Evening with You

*How beautiful you are, my love, how beautiful! Your eyes are*
*soft as doves'. What a lovely, pleasant thing you are, lying here*
*upon the grass, shaded by the cedar trees and firs.*

SONG OF SOLOMON 1:15 TLB

My Dear Husband,

I love just being with you. We don't have to dine at the Ritz, dance until
dawn, or even canoe across a moonlit bay. A romantic evening doesn't need
to cost a fortune, take hours of time, or require formal wear. Sometimes it's
better, and more romantic, just to keep it simple.

Sometimes all I want is a quiet evening with just you and me, alone—
together at home. Maybe we can fix a simple meal together (and who knows
what can happen in a kitchen?). Or maybe we can take a neighborhood
stroll, quietly holding hands as we go. Or perhaps we'll play Scrabble, and
I'll let you win for a change. But whatever we do, let's just do it
together—the two of us.

Dear God, remind us to plan quiet times—intimate moments for just
the two of us—into the busyness of our lives. Help us to remember that the
most important thing is to be together. Amen.

# Seize the Day!

**This is the day that the LORD has made;
let us rejoice and be glad in it.**

PSALM 118:24 NIV

⁓⊙⁓

*My Dear Husband,*

*I love your spontaneity. Sometimes I get so focused on the demanding details of life—ordinary things like laundry and carpools and deadlines— that I completely forget to savor the precious moments of living. And sometimes I need a gentle, but firm, reminder to pause from all my endless activity and to stop and smell the roses—to seize the day.*

*For only God knows how many earthly days we have to spend together—or how many moments we are allowed where we can embrace and speak those sweet words of love and affection to one another. And when it's all said and done, we'll never regret such pleasant times. So, let's remind each other to enjoy this time we have together—to cherish each new day as a true gift from God.*

⁓⊙⁓

*Dear God, only You know the span of our lives—but whether they're short or long, each day is unique and special and worthy of celebration. Teach us to celebrate each one. Amen.*

# Let's Take a Walk

*The leaves are coming out and the grape vines are in blossom.*
*How delicious they smell! Arise, my love, my fair one,*
*and come away.*

SONG OF SOLOMON 2:13 TLB

My Dear Husband,

I love being by your side. There's something so exquisite about taking a stroll with the one you love. The warm comforting feeling of holding hands. The relaxing sense of moving along, unhurried. The simplicity of enjoying the weather, appreciating the landscape, and the leisurely rhythm of two pairs of footsteps falling into a gentle pace—almost like dancing.

So, let's take a walk together, my love. Let's breathe deeply of the fresh air and appreciate this rejuvenation of our spirits, a refreshing of our souls. Whether we visit quietly as we go or simply listen to the quietness—drinking in the sounds of birds sweetly singing or the gentle breeze as it ripples over the land—I know we will enjoy being together.

Dear God, simple pleasures always seem to be the best. Remind us to take time to enjoy them together. Amen.

# A Five-Minute Exercise

*Before the dawn comes and the shadows flee away,*
*come back to me, my love.*

SONG OF SOLOMON 2:17 NLT

∽◑◐∾

My Dear Husband,

I love the feel of your hands. I love their confidence, their sureness, their adeptness. I love the assurance I feel when you touch me. I feel so connected to you. Now this might sound a little corny (at first), but please hear me out. You see, I think we sometimes get so comfortable around each other that we forget to notice the little things—or maybe we've started to take one another just a little for granted. So some evening, when it's all quiet and calm, let's do this simple exercise together.

Let's sit on the floor (cross-legged, if we can), and let's face each other and reach out and touch our palms together, just lightly. And then without speaking, let's just look into each other's face—and I'll try not to giggle. First let's enjoy the sensation of touching palms, then let's close our eyes and "read" each other's faces with our fingertips.

───────── ∽◑◐∾ ─────────

Dear God, show us creative ways to open wonderful new doors in our relationship, allowing us to see one another in a fresh new way. Amen.

# When You Support Me

*I will sing of your strength,*
*in the morning I will sing of your love;*
*for you are my fortress,*
*my refuge in times of trouble.*

PSALM 59:16 NIV

❦

My Dear Husband,

I love how you back me up. Sometimes I really want to try something new, take on a fresh challenge, or expand my everyday world just a little. But it can be pretty scary to step out, and I'm not always as confident as I try to appear. The truth is, it almost always seems easier to just do nothing. Perhaps you understand what I'm trying to say.

It's those times—times when one of us is facing a challenge—that we really need to support one another. When I step out into a new area, it means everything to me to know that you are standing behind me, backing me, cheering me on. Your encouragement means more to me than you can possibly imagine. I want to be there for you in the same way—urging, supporting, cheering.

---

Dear God, teach us to be cheerleaders for each other, helping us both to become all that You have called us to be. Amen.

# Realizing Our Dreams

*Help me to do your will, for you are my God.*
*Lead me in good paths,*
*for your Spirit is good.*

PSALM 143:10 TLB

ᥴᥱᥰᥱᥲ

*My* Dear Husband,

*I love it when our dreams come true. Let's dream together, my love. Let's talk about our hopes and aspirations for the future—whether they seem realistic or not. Let's discuss where we want to be and how we'd like to get there. Then let's consider ways to make goals and strategies.*

*Let's not be afraid to dream big. Or to dream small. And let's not be afraid to have our dreams change—for we are constantly changing.*

*But most of all, let's be sure to pray for God's guidance and direction. And let's ask God to enhance and expand our dreams to match all that He has planned for us. Who knows, He may choose to give us completely new dreams. Wouldn't that be exciting!*

ᥴᥱᥰᥱᥲ

*Dear God, teach us to dream Your dreams—and to dream them together. Then show us ways of implementing those dreams, and help us to realize them within our lifetime. Amen.*

# Just Tell Me You Love Me

*He has brought me to his banquet hall,*
*And his banner over me is love. . . .*
*I am my beloved's and my beloved is mine.*

SONG OF SOLOMON 2:4, 6:3 NAS

*My Dear Husband,*

*I bless you for telling me. Oh, sure, I know they are just words—three little words at that. But they mean so much. I love to hear you whisper them in my ear, those wonderful words, "I love you." They are the life and substance of our relationship. Those words lift me up when I'm down; they heal my spirit when I feel wounded. Those words keep me going when I feel that I can't. Those words are a lifeline for me. And I will never tire of hearing you say those three words, "I love you."*

*I promise to remember to say them to you as well—never to let you go one day without hearing them. They are my pledge of faith to you, renewed day by day. They represent our covenant, the certainty of our union. They are more precious than gold.*

---

*Dear God, help us never to forget to say those three little words, "I love you." They mean so much. Amen.*

# Let's Make a Plan

**The LORD will guide you always; he will satisfy your needs in a
sun-scorched land and will strengthen your frame.
You will be like a well-watered garden,
like a spring whose waters never fail.**

ISAIAH 58:11 NIV

❧

My Dear Husband,

I bless you taking time. Sometimes it's good to sit down together and
make a simple plan—whether it's for a vacation, a weekend away, a
home—improvement project, or simply next week's shopping list. Whatever
the task, it can be fun and fulfilling to make plans, together with you. And
it's rewarding to share ideas and to cooperate with each other. Sure, I know
it can try our patience sometimes, but it also teaches us how to give and
take—and it improves our listening skills.

It feels so good when we accomplish what we've set out to do. It's
exciting to know that we have learned to work together as a team.

❧

Dear God, show us new and different ways to plan and carry out
our plans together. We know it won't all go smoothly, but we believe it will be
well worth the effort. Amen.

# What's Really Important

*"You must love the Lord your God with all your heart, all your*
*soul, all your strength, and all your mind."*
*And, "Love your neighbor as yourself."*

LUKE 10:27 NLT

⤮⤯

*My Dear Husband,*

*I love that you think I'm important. There are so many pulls and
demands on my life and on yours, too. And sometimes the most urgent
things appear to be the most important. I often find myself giving those
pressing issues my top priority. But if I would only step back and take a
couple of deep breaths, I might just realize that they're not so important
after all.*

*If I pause to think about it, I'm often reminded of what's truly
important in life. And it's usually quite simple—embarrassingly simple.
And, because I love you, I want to remind you, too. First of all, I know
it's vitally important for me to love God with my whole heart, to love and
cherish you, to love myself, and to love others—in that order. That's the
road to true happiness.*

⤮⤯

*Dear God, thank You for reminding us to keep our priorities straight
and simple and to escape the tyranny of the urgent. Amen.*

# Let's Share a Book

*Make your ear attentive to wisdom.*
*Incline your heart to understanding.*

PROVERBS 2:2 NAS

☙֍֎

My Dear Husband,

Your intelligence is valuable to me. I know our tastes differ in some areas, but I think it's possible to find some common ground in literature—if we're willing to try, that is, and willing to compromise a little. So, let's go together and select a good book, one that we'll both want to read and enjoy. It can be a novel, a biography, a how-to, or whatever—as long as we both agree. And then let's read the book together.

Perhaps we could take turns reading aloud to each other at bedtime. Or maybe we could each read the same chapter, separately, and discuss it later. Maybe we should read the entire book and then talk about it, discussing what we liked and what we didn't. What do you think?

☙֍֎

Dear God, it's important to bring our minds together so that we can experience something new and grow as individuals and as a couple. Help us to find a book to read together that will bless us both. Amen.

# What Are Your Dreams?

*Every day and all night long their counsel will lead you and save you from harm; when you wake up in the morning, let their instructions guide you into the new day.*

PROVERBS 6:22 TLB

My Dear Husband,

Your dreams are important to me. Do you have some secret dreams hidden away in your heart? Perhaps they've been sleeping there since childhood and might even seem silly to you now. Or maybe they're recent dreams, but they seem too impossible or unlikely to be shared with someone else. Or maybe even too wild and ridiculous to mention out loud.

But you can tell me, my love. Even if they're strange things like wanting to join the circus, or leap out of high-flying airplanes, or play drums in a rock 'n' roll band, I still want to hear all about them. And I promise to try to be a good listener. So, trust me and consider sharing your aspirations. Please tell me your dreams.

---

Dear God, continue to teach us how important trust is to our marriage. Give us the courage to share our dreams with You and with each other. Amen.

# Your Strong Hands

**We are His workmanship, created in Christ Jesus for good
works, which God prepared beforehand
that we should walk in them.**

EPHESIANS 2:10 NKJV

*My Dear Husband,*

*I bless you for your touch. I love your hands. I love their strength and
power, I love their tender gentleness. I love the feel of your fingers wrapping
themselves securely around my own. I love the warm squeezes you give to
support and encourage me during a difficult time. I love the kindness I see
when your hands reach out to help someone. And I love to see your hands
picking up a small child. I just love your hands.*

*I love when your fingers gently massage the tight muscles in the back of
my neck. How I love the way you affectionately tousle my hair. And I love
the feel of your index finger slowly tracing the curve of my cheek. Your
hands are a symbol of your love for me, and oh, how I treasure them.*

---

*Dear God, thank You for the wonderful connection that we can make
through touch. It is a gift from You. Thank You for the gentleness and strength
that touch conveys. Amen.*

# I Know What You're Thinking

**When my anxious thoughts multiply within me,
Your consolations delight my soul.**

PSALM 94:19 NAS

*My* Dear Husband,

Your thoughts intrigue me. Now, don't worry, for it doesn't happen all the time. And honestly, I don't claim to be clairvoyant or some kind of mystical mind reader. But sometimes, my love, I think I know what you're thinking. And occasionally I hear your words before they touch your lips. Maybe it's because we've been together awhile, or we're just in sync.

It's not a bad thing, not at all. It's probably just the inevitable reward of two people loving each other like we do. And it brings me joy to know what's on your mind. So, don't take offense the next time I say, "I knew you were going to say that." But rejoice that our hearts and minds are becoming one.

---

*Dear* God, continue to knit our lives together, help our hearts and minds to unite in understanding. It's Your divine will that two become one in Your love. Amen.

# Home Matters

**Therefore everyone who hears these words of mine and puts them into practice is like a wise man who built his house on the rock.**

MATTHEW 7:24 NIV

ଚ୭ଚ୭ଚ

*M*y Dear Husband,

I bless you for our home. Some say that a house is more important to a woman because it's more of a reflection on her than on her husband. But I've come to believe that it's a more true reflection of us—a visual aid that spotlights the condition of our relationship. When our marriage functions well, I think our home runs more smoothly. And if the home front is lagging, perhaps we need to invest more time in our relationship.

I long to have a warm and open home where we both feel at ease and comfortable, but I can't do it without you. So, take a look around our home. Is it all that it could be—or is there room for improvement? Let's start with what really matters–us.

ଚ୭ଚ୭ଚ

*D*ear God, give us the grace to partner together to make our home a true reflection of our marriage. Help us to appreciate elements like warmth, beauty, and comfort, and make our hearts feel at home. Amen.

# Worshiping Together

*Oh come, let us worship and bow down;*
*Let us kneel before the LORD our Maker.*
*For He is our God,*
*And we are the people of His pasture,*
*And the sheep of His hand.*

PSALM 95:6-7 NKJV

My Dear Husband,

I love when we both look to God. Such amazing things happen when I stand next to you and we worship God. Whether we're praying together amidst the congregation, or singing hymns with the choir, or silently worshiping in the pew—something totally unexpected and incredible takes place inside my heart. For whenever we worship God together, with honest and open spirits, I feel closer to you than ever.

So, let's take advantage of these opportunities to worship with each other. Let's make sure we take time to attend services and gather together with other believers. And let's remind ourselves that one day we will bow before the throne of God and worship at His feet—still standing side by side.

*Dear God, teach us to come together before You—to honor and worship and praise You. Unite our hearts as never before. Amen.*

# Looking Ahead

**A house is built by wisdom and becomes strong through good sense. Through knowledge its rooms are filled with all sorts of precious riches and valuables.**

PROVERBS 24:3-4 NLT

∽◌◌◌◌∾

*M*y Dear Husband,

*I love looking forward with you. Building our marriage is a lot like building a house. If we take the time and invest the energy, it should protect and sustain us through the oncoming years. And when I consider the future, I smile as I imagine us growing older together, getting closer, our relationship deepening with time. I think a love like ours can only improve with age.*

*Like a beautifully built older home, with mature landscaping and a beautiful patina to the woodwork, I imagine our marriage growing more and more lovely with each passing year. But like an older home, I know we'll need to continue doing careful maintenance—for neglect can lead to ruin. But our reward will be a wonderful haven of love.*

∽◌◌◌◌∾

*D*ear God, *teach us to recognize the everyday increasing value of our marriage. Show us how to care for it as if it were a priceless investment—which, in fact, it is. Amen.*

# Are You Really from Mars?

**Take a look at the hippopotamus!
I made him, too, just as I made you!**

JOB 40:15 TLB

My Dear Husband,

I bless you for being different. There's a rumor going around that you're from Mars and I'm from Venus, but I happen to believe we're both the by-products of God's amazing creativity combined with His wonderful sense of humor. Although, to be honest, sometimes it can seem as if we actually came from two entirely different worlds.

Let's learn to treat our differences with the same dignity we would show a foreign guest. Instead of conforming a visitor to our traditions and culture, we would more likely express interest and respect for his ways and try to learn from him. So let's appreciate our differing perspectives and unique backgrounds—and let's learn from each other. Your masculinity and my feminity were custom-made by God.

Dear God, forgive us for the times we have failed to appreciate the differences You've placed within us. Help us to see each other with new eyes. Amen.

# Mixed Memories

*For who sees anything different in you? What do you have that you did not receive? And if you received it, why do you boast as if it were not a gift?*

1 CORINTHIANS 4:7 NRSV

∞⊙⊙∞

*M*y Dear Husband,

*I bless you for how you see things. Do you remember what I was wearing when we first met? Do you remember the color? Do you recall what you were wearing? Well, we don't always remember things in the same way, do we?*

*Perhaps it's because our memories latch onto different things and neither one of us is completely right or completely wrong. Consider two people describing the same house (one from inside and one from outside). One says the house is blue and one says the house is white—and though their opinions differ, they're both right. I think we could learn a lot by comparing notes.*

———————————— ∞⊙⊙∞ ————————————

*D*ear God, help us not only to respect our different perspectives, but to enjoy the varied interest we both bring to this marriage. Thank You for our uniqueness. Amen.

# On Those Special Days

*Shout joyfully to the LORD, all the earth;*
*Break forth and sing for joy and sing praises.*

PSALM 98:4 NAS

&

*My Dear Husband,*

*Thank you for remembering. Throughout the year, holidays and birthdays and various celebrations occur. And I've come to realize that due to our unique backgrounds and upbringings, we view these momentous occasions differently. We both bring a differing set of expectations and customs to our marriage. I admit that I sometimes forget this important fact. Whether we open presents Christmas Eve or Christmas morning, for example, isn't so important as that we celebrate together and create new customs. We can have the best of both worlds!*

*Forgive me if I've frustrated and even disappointed you when these special days have not gone the way you expected them to. Let's agree to discuss and plan these times well in advance. And let's both be willing to compromise as we build our own new traditions.*

---

*Dear God, we lay all our hopes and expectations before You. Help us to plan together to make the most of those special times and to draw closer to You and to each other as a result. Amen.*

# Sometimes I Watch You

*Like an apple tree among the trees of the forest,*
*So is my beloved among the young men.*
*In his shade I took great delight and sat down,*
*And his fruit was sweet to my taste.*

SONG OF SOLOMON 2:3 NAS

᎐᠗᠍᠍᠍᠍᠗᠍᠗᠍᠗

My Dear Husband,

I love what I see in you. I like to watch you when you're interacting with someone else, or intently focusing on a favorite hobby, or sometimes simply sleeping. I like to study your face—the little lines that are beginning to appear around your eyes, the shape of your nose, the curve of your earlobe, the jat of your chin.

But even more than that, I like to watch your facial expressions—the way your brow slightly furrows with concern when you see a friend in some sort of difficulty. Or the way you grow thoughtful when someone asks a provoking question. Or how the corners of your mouth curl up just before you laugh.

---

*Dear God, thank You for the little things that we enjoy so much about each other. Thank You for the love that makes those things so special. Amen.*

# When I'm Tired

*Your love has given me great joy and encouragement,
because you, brother, have refreshed
the hearts of the saints.*

PHILEMON 1:7 NIV

~∞✺∞~

*My Dear Husband,*

*I bless you for your help. Life's stresses and demands can take their toll on me. And sometimes I just get plain tired and fatigued. Like an engine running on empty, I start to slow down and lag behind, and sometimes I don't even realize how it all happened or even why.*

*It's times like these when I really need you. I need your patience and your understanding and your gentle encouragement. Perhaps I even need you to encourage me to slow down and rest or to point out how I've been neglecting myself in my frenzy to keep on going. Because the truth is, I often do put my needs after everyone else's—and a loving reminder from you can prevent me from getting weary.*

———————— ~∞✺∞~ ————————

*Dear God, help us to be sensitive to the weariness and fatigue that comes as a result of giving ourselves to those we love. Help us to watch over each other with care and to gently remind each other to rest. Amen.*

# You Make Me Complete

*In the same way, we are many, but in Christ we are all one body.
Each one is a part of that body, and each part
belongs to all the other parts.*

ROMANS 12:5 NCV

ᙨᙩᙪ

My Dear Husband,

I love what I learn from you. Okay, it's not as if I don't consider
myself a whole and entire person—because I know that I am. But on the
other hand, I believe that being married to you somehow makes me more
complete. It's hard to understand or even explain how this little miracle
actually works. I think it just must be another one of God's great
mysteries. But just the same, I'm so thankful for it.

For you've stretched me in all kinds of areas—the way nothing else ever
could. And as I live and learn in our relationship, I honestly believe I
become a "bigger" person—more loving, forgiving, and kind. And I hope I
do the same for you.

ᙨᙩᙪ

Dear God, thank You for putting us together, for seeing that we would
be good for each other. We know we are both better people because we are
together and we appreciate it. Amen.

# Let's Turn Down the Lights

*My beloved is like a gazelle or a young stag.*
*Look, there he stands behind our wall,*
*gazing in at the windows, looking through the lattice.*

SONG OF SOLOMON 2:9 NRSV

ℳy Dear Husband,

I bless you for our romance. Something magical happens when you turn the lights down low—especially when there's a soft glow of candlelight combined with sweet tones of music. Haven't you noticed how a romantic hush can settle over a dimly lit room, how the shadows can magically obscure the distractions and simply push them far away from us?

Suddenly it's just you and me—alone together—in our undisturbed little world. You become my focus and I become yours. And we can take the time to sit together, enjoying quiet and intimate conversation, sweet nuances, the pleasure of familiarity, the expectation of things to come. So, turn down the lights, my love.

---

𝒟ear God, help us never to minimize the need for romance in our relationship. It reminds us that we need each other and that we enjoy the pleasure of being together. Amen.

# I'm Here for You

*Though one might prevail against another,*
*two will withstand one.*
*A threefold cord is not quickly broken.*

ECCLESIASTES 4:12 NRSV

❧

My Dear Husband,

I love cheering you on. I think there's a tiny part of every little girl that wants to become a cheerleader. And, who knows, maybe that's the way God made us—so that one day we could stand up and cheer on our man, bolstering him with our support and encouragement. That's the way I want to cheer you on. I want to clap my hands and say, "Go, fight, win!" And you know what? You will!

I'm here for you, my love. I'm standing behind you (and beside you). I hope and believe the very best for you and your life. Your success is my success (and mine, yours). By the same token, your disappointment is also mine. So whatever happens, for better or for worse, I am here for you.

❧

Dear God, we thank You for placing us together. This life would be so lonely if we had to face it alone. What a powerfully victorious team the three of us can be. Amen.

# Sometimes I Get Busy

*It will be a sign between me and the Israelites forever, for in six days the LORD made the heavens and the earth, and on the seventh day he abstained from work and rested.*

EXODUS 31:17 NIV

ده‌ودو

*My* Dear Husband,

I bless you for your patient reminders. Life occasionally gets pretty hectic around here, and sometimes I literally can't remember if I'm coming or going. It often seems I've got a dozen things to take care of—all at once—and that's before breakfast! When I get busy and distracted with the demanding details of life, I sometimes forget to communicate very carefully, or thoughtfully, and I can become impatient. And in my heart, I'm sorry.

You can help me, during these stressful times by gently reminding me to slow down and keep my priorities in order. I welcome your tender correction, for it is my desire to be the best wife I can be to you and to be a blessing to your life.

———————————— ده‌ودو ————————————

*Dear* God, we all get busy sometimes and it's difficult to say "no." Help us to gently remind each other to slow down when the busyness gets too great. Amen.

# When I Think of You

*I am sending him to you for the express purpose
that you may know about our circumstances
and that he may encourage your hearts.*

COLOSSIANS 4:8 NIV

*My Dear Husband,*

*Just the thought of you warms me. Sometimes in the midst of a trying situation, or if it seems the whole world has turned against me, you come to mind. And when I think of you, I am comforted and encouraged. Maybe it's because I can imagine your strong arms around me, or I can envision your smile, or I can hear you whisper sweet words of love and kindness into my ear.*

*Somehow, just thinking of you brings a quiet sense of peace and joy to my heart. And then I instantly grow thankful that you and I will come back together at the end of the day. I know how you'll listen to my tales of woe and how you'll console me, and maybe we'll laugh about the whole silly thing together. Thank you for loving me.*

*Dear God, the world is a warmer, friendlier place because we have each other. Thank You for giving us the ability to comfort one another. Amen.*

# I Need Your Love

**Now faith, hope, love, abide these three;
but the greatest of these is love.**

1 CORINTHIANS 13:13 NAS

*My* Dear Husband,

I bless you for your tender love. I'm always declaring one kind of need or another. How often I need your help with mundane, but necessary, things like taking out the trash, getting the car checked, or cleaning the gutters. And then sometimes I simply need you to hold my hand, to stroke my hair, or to tell me everything's going to be okay.

But I don't usually admit how much I need your love. I think there's something inside us that doesn't like to acknowledge such deeply felt needs. Maybe we're afraid of what might happen if those needs were denied. But the fact is, I need your love—desperately. Your love means everthing to me. Without it, I would be nothing.

---

*Dear* God, love is the lifeblood of our marriage. We need Your love and the love we bring to each other. Remind us to always give our love freely. Amen.

# Accepting My Friends

*Do not forsake your own friend or your father's friend,*
*And do not go to your brother's house*
*in the day of your calamity;*
*Better is a neighbor who is near than a brother far away.*

PROVERBS 27:10 NAS

⁓⊙⊙⌇

*My Dear Husband,*

*Thank you for being gracious. Okay, let's be honest and admit it—my friends aren't always your friends. Nor are yours mine. And although it can sometimes be a bone of contention, I think we can get past it, if we try. Because the fact is, just as you and I are different (and we're learning to accept and appreciate those differences), so our friends are different, too.*

*I make this commitment to you now: I will try to see the good in each of your friends. I will work hard to understand why each of these friends is so important to you, what each one brings to your life. I hope you will do the same for me. I know we will be happier when we see the good in every person who is part of our lives.*

⁓⊙⊙⌇

*Dear God, help us not to be jealous or resent the friends You put in each of our lives. Give us an honest appreciation for them. Remind us that You love each person. Amen.*

# A Friendly Face

**A cheerful look brings joy to the heart;
good news makes for good health.**

PROVERBS 15:30 NLT

❧

*M*y Dear Husband,

   *I love to see your smile. You know how you can be having one of those really crummy days where no matter how hard you try, nothing ever goes right, and it starts to feels as if that day will never end? So often when that happens to me, out of the blue, you call me just to say, "I love you." Or, even better, you show up. And suddenly, there you are just smiling at me—and somehow when I see your friendly, grinning face, it assures me that I can make it.*

   *I also love it when we go to a place full of people I don't even know and who don't seem eager to know me, and I spot your face in the crowd. Oh, how I appreciate that, especially when you look right into my eyes and smile. Your love is my most cherished possession.*

❧

   *D*ear God, a smiling and friendly face is like a healthy tonic. It refreshes and invigorates the soul. Help us always to appreciate the gift You have given us as we look into each other's welcoming eyes. Amen.

# You're My Best Friend

*There are "friends" who pretend to be friends,
but there is a friend who
sticks closer than a brother.*

PROVERBS 18:24 TLB

*My Dear Husband,*

*I bless you for your friendship. It's no secret that strong friendships fortify the best of marriages. And when I see a couple who enjoys the same kinds of activities and each other's company, I suspect they have a relationship destined to go the distance. And that's what I desire for us. I want to be your very best friend, and I want you to be mine.*

*I know it takes time and commitment to be best friends, but I believe it's worth it. I want to be that sort of dependable friend to you. So, let's agree to set our friendship above all others. Let's come together with honest and caring hearts. Let's pursue common interests and spend plenty of quality time together.*

---

*Dear God, please help us build a lasting friendship. Teach us about commitment and love, show us ways to develop similar interests, and join our hearts as friends. Amen.*

# Fanning the Flame

*Let him kiss me with the kisses of his mouth—*
*For your love is better than wine.*

SONG OF SOLOMON 1:2 NKJV

*My* Dear Husband,

I bless you for the heat of your love. What do you do when passion's embers burn low? Do you know how to fan the flame of romance back into a hotly burning fire? Which reminds me how someone once said that true romance begins in the kitchen (of course, if you can't take the heat, you better stay out). So, my love, let's be certain to ignite romance in every room by doing those things that keep love burning brightly.

Don't you agree that true romance begins with a kind and caring attitude? It can start with gentleness and helping hands. Maybe it's a look of appreciation, a thoughtful word, or a tender touch. And like some recipes, it must slowly simmer before coming to a boil. So let's gently fan the flame and see what we can cook up.

*Dear* God, teach us how to be kind and good to one another, always remembering that love is strongest when it is given away. Amen.

# I Believe in You

**Many people claim to be loyal, but it is hard to find a trustworthy person.
The good people who live honest lives
will be a blessing to their children.**

PROVERBS 20:6-7 NCV

*My Dear Husband,*

*I bless your success. I know you're not perfect—just as you know that I'm not. I probably know more about your mistakes than anyone on earth. And yet, I surely love you more than any other person does except God! Why?*

*It's because I believe in you. I believe that you're a truly wonderful person. I believe that you will succeed at whatever you put your mind to. I believe in your diligence, your strength, your intelligence, your heart, and much more. And I will always believe in you, my love. You are destined for great things.*

*Dear God, teach us to trust You more by believing in each other. And though this kind of trust can make us feel vulnerable, we know we can rely on You to sustain us through all things. Amen.*

# Let's Make Some Time

**To everything there is a season,
A time for every purpose under heaven.**

ECCLESIASTES 3:1 NKJV

⌘

*My Dear Husband,*

*Thanks for valuing our time together. How often do we say we'll do this or that or that we'll go here or there "when we have the time"? But time seems to pass so quickly. Before we realize it, the time is gone and we haven't done any of the things we meant to do. So instead of waiting until we have the time——et's decide right here and now to make the time, and then let's take the time to do those things we've talked about.*

*Let's sit down with our calendars and make a plan together. Let's block out time that belongs only to us—to our relationship—to our marriage. Whether it's a few days away, a weekly date-night, or a meeting for lunch—let's get it in writing and commit to do it. Our love is worth making time for.*

⌘

*Dear God, only You know how many days we have together in this life. Help us to be wise, plan ahead, make the time we need, and then take it and enjoy it.*

# Something You Don't Know

*Can you fathom the mysteries of God?*
*Can you probe the limits of the Almighty?*
*They are higher than the heavens.*

JOB 11:7-8 NIV

*My Dear Husband,*

*I love that we've more to learn. Do you think you know everything about me? Well, I've got good news. There are still some things you don't know, things we've never yet discussed, areas still waiting to be explored. And by the same token, I'm sure there are some places in you where I've never been.*

*These are places that will take a lifetime to uncover. Things that should be revealed slowly, with the greatest amount of trust. The more I learn about you, the more I love you. But isn't that the wonderful mystery of our relationship—that even after all the time we've been together, we still have some unexplored territory to discover?*

---

*Dear God, thank You for making us infinitely interesting to each other. It will take a lifetime to reveal all the mysteries of who we are to one another. How delightful that will be. Amen.*

# Let's Dance

*You will again be happy and dance merrily with timbrels.*

JEREMIAH 31:4 TLB

*My Dear Husband,*

*I love it when we celebrate our love. Let's listen to some really good music—something we both like—something that makes us want to get onto our feet and move to its rhythm. It can be fast and energetic, or it can be slow and soulful. But let's allow the music to flow right through us, and then let's cast our inhibitions aside, and let's dance. You can be my Fred, and I will be your Ginger. You lead so well in the rest of our lives, and I want to follow your lead on the dance floor as well.*

*Before the night is over, let's make sure we dance real slowly. I want to feel the warmth of your body and the security of your arms around me as we sway gently, moving together. For our souls seem to meld as our feet move us across the floor. Come on, baby, let's dance.*

---

*Dear God, thank You for the fun of spending time together and with You. For laughter and happy times, for warmth and security, for energy and soul, we thank You. Amen.*

# Total Truth

*Instead, speaking the truth in love, we will in all things grow up into him who is the Head, that is, Christ.*

EPHESIANS 4:15 NIV

*My Dear Husband,*

*I love your honesty with me. Any healthy relationship has a solid foundation of openness and honesty beneath it. And that's what I long for with us. I want you to always feel you can be completely candid with me, even if it's not totally comfortable. For how can we grow and change in our relationship if we shy away from the truth? And doesn't the truth, after all, set us free?*

*But let's remember not to use honesty as an excuse to bluntly wound each other. Let's keep in mind that love must always accompany truth—that truth without love can be painful. And let's also agree to quietly listen to the truth, even when it hurts—and then we can allow time to process it, believing that the end results are well worth it.*

*Dear God, we need honesty in our relationship. Show us how to speak the truth in love, teach us to react with wisdom and dignity, and help us to grow closer together. Amen.*

# When We Pray Together

*Therefore I say to you, all things for which you pray and ask,*
*believe that you have received them,*
*and they will be granted you.*

MARK 11:24 NAS

*My Dear Husband,*

*I love that our hearts can agree in prayer. It's certainly not the easiest thing to do. And it seems there are always a dozen reasons why we can't and don't—it's too late, too early, or we're too busy, too tired. For some reason, it's just easier not to pray together. But here's the amazing thing: When we actually do sit down and really pray together, something incredible happens in our hearts and souls. It seems we are bound together in power and in strength, and our spirits unite and we become one.*

*Just the same, it can be difficult for me to ask you to pray. For some reason I tend to wait, hoping you will lead the way. Together, let's discover the best ways we can join our hearts in prayer. And then, no excuses, let's just do it.*

---

*Dear God, help us come together to decide how we can become better prayer partners, whether with a prayer list or in silent prayer. Show us the way. Amen.*

# I'm Lost without You

*He saves them from death and spares
their lives in times of hunger.
So our hope is in the LORD.
He is our help, our shield to protect us.*

PSALM 33:19-20 NCV

*My* Dear Husband,

I love that you're my true north. Of course, I like you to think I'm a
fairly independent person—able to confidently handle and conquer most
parts of my day with little or no help. But the truth is, if you're away
from home for just a day or two, I begin to feel rather lost without you. I
notice your absence during all my waking moments. But to be honest, I'm
relieved to feel this way.

For when I'm missing you like that, I realize how connected our lives
truly are. And I become acutely aware of how important you are to me
and how empty my life would be without you in it. I need you sleeping
beside me. I need your smile to start my day. I need your hand around
mine. I'm lost without you.

*Dear* God, thank You for reminding us that we need each other. Help
us to always appreciate the fact that You have placed us together. Amen.

# How Do I Love Thee?

*Tell me, O you whom I love,*
*Where you feed your flock,*
*Where you make it rest at noon.*

SONG OF SOLOMON 1:7 NKJV

*My Dear Husband,*

I love so much about you. Some people count their blessings to help them go to sleep. But sometimes I think I might try to count how many things I love about you—for that's a blessing in itself. For starters, I love the feel of your touch when you stroke my hair. And I love the twinkle in your eye when we share a private joke. I love how you call me up sometimes just to hear my voice.

I love the strength of your arm wrapped securely around my waist. I love how your hand envelops mine as we walk along. I love the shape of your mouth as it curves into a smile. I love the hearty sound of your laugh. And like the song goes, "I love how you love me."

---

*Dear God, we ask You to help make our love grow like a well-watered garden in springtime. We ask that You'll show us new ways to share and communicate our love for each other. Amen.*

# When We Are Old

**White hair is a crown of glory
and is seen most among the godly.**

PROVERBS 16:31 TLB

༺ⓖ༻

*My Dear Husband,*

*I love imagining you in the future. Sometimes I try to imagine us with white, wispy hair and parchment skin, our bodies slightly bent by the passing of years. And I wonder, will our love still be as fresh and young as it was on the day we repeated our wedding vows? I ponder how a fragile thing like love can endure the effects of time and years—how it can survive the hurts and misunderstandings which occur living life. And I wonder if our passion can remain unhampered by aging?*

*To be honest, I sometimes see myself—the aging process already in motion—and I wonder, will you still love me as wrinkles deepen, age spots appear, and the inevitable pull of gravity makes my body sag. I need your assurance—tell me your love is here to stay.*

༺ⓖ༻

*Dear God, we're all getting older. Remind us that our love for each other is based on who we are and not on how we look. Amen.*

# Distractions Come

**I am sending you out as sheep among wolves. Be as wary as serpents and harmless as doves.**

MATTHEW 10:16 TLB

*My Dear Husband,*

*I bless you for focusing our love. As we move through life, we are constantly bombarded with all kinds of distractions. They come in various shapes and forms—anything from a pesky phone call to demanding work projects, family crises, or the daily needs of those around us. And occasionally these distractions will try to steal our focus from our marriage and take us in a completely different direction. That's when we need to be on our guard.*

*So, let's agree together to prevent distractions from turning into divisions that would come between us and separate us. Let's carefully gauge which distractions have the painful potential to divide—and then let's learn to quickly step away.*

---

*Dear God, help us to be wise as we navigate through life. Give us discernment for the distracting dangers that would divide us in our marriage, and help us to obey. Amen.*

# God's Touch on Our Lives

*I will send you the Helper
from the Father.*

JOHN 15:26 NCV

*My* Dear Husband,

I see God shaping our relationship. I believe it happens regularly—as we move through our day, taking care of life's responsibilities, trying to do what's right, working to get ahead—it's God's touch on our lives. It's those delectable little moments when God quietly administers His wonderful gifts of grace, protection, mercy, or love into our everyday routine. Where would we be without God's touch? I wonder how many times we forget to even pause and take notice.

And I can see God's touch on our marriage, too—ways that He has preserved and watched over us. It's amazing how He continually knits our hearts together, how He strengthens our love and even teaches us to forgive each other. So, let's take time to acknowledge Him.

*Dear* God, we thank You and praise You for your faithful touch upon our lives. Please, help us not to take Your love for granted. We know our marriage is a gift from Your hand. Amen.

# When We Give Gifts

*You are generous because of your faith. And I am praying that
you will really put your generosity to work,
for in so doing you will come to an understanding
of all the good things we can do for Christ.*

PHILEMON 1:6 NLT

⁓⊙⊙⊙⁓

*M*y Dear Husband,

*I bless you for your generosity. Isn't it a wonderful delight to be able to
give someone a special gift? Something about the act of being generous really
lifts my spirits and invigorates my heart. And I do believe that those of us
fortunate enough to be on the giving end truly do attain the very best part
of the blessing—for being able to give is better than to receive.*

*But I think the act of giving is even more fulfilling when we can do it
together, as a couple. So let's talk about some ways we can give to others—
ways we can share from the abundance of our lives, from our happiness,
from our material wealth. And then let's live generously and enjoy the thrill
of giving and blessing others.*

⁓⊙⊙⊙⁓

*D*ear God, teach us to live and to give with a generous spirit. Show us
those who are in need and ways we can bless them with the abundance You've
so graciously poured into our lives. Amen.*

# Quiet Moments

*Be still, and know that I am God;*
*I will be exalted among the nations,*
*I will be exalted in the earth!*

PSALM 46:10 NKJV

My Dear Husband,

I love being "still" with you. Sometimes my spirit hungers for a special place of calm and peace and quiet. And I long for an undisturbed portion of time when I can simply bask in God's love and grace, perhaps even enjoying a perfect slice of His beautiful creation while I'm at it. And how I'd love to share some of those delectable moments with you.

So, how about it? Can we plan for some pleasant moments like that? Just spending quiet time together, doing something we both enjoy, but without the need to fill up all the time and space with words or activity? Instead, can we just allow our spirits an undisturbed period of peaceful interlude—just you and me and God?

---

Dear God, show us some special ways to spend a quiet time together. Teach us to come to You consistently, to savor Your peace and calm, and to be refreshed together. Amen.

# We Both Change

*And do not be conformed to this world, but be transformed by the renewing of your mind, so that you may prove what the will of God is, that which is good and acceptable and perfect.*

ROMANS 12:2 NAS

*My* Dear Husband,

I bless you for accepting changes. It's as inevitable as the passing of time. For as the years steadily come and go, we change. But to stay the same would be to stagnate, to cease growing, and to eventually die. And so as life comes pushing at us from all angles, we do change—hopefully we become more like God. But some changes are hard to accept. Sometimes our human nature just wants everything to remain the same. But it doesn't.

So let's remember that change really is good. And as we watch each other changing and growing over the years, let's applaud these transitions, and let's welcome these new seasons of life. Let's learn to embrace change with wide-open arms.

*Dear* God, You alone are changeless—Your love and grace and kindness remain a constant throughout the ages. But we are in continual transition. We pray that You will change us to be more like You. Amen.

# A Warm Embrace

*You have ravished my heart, my lovely one, my bride; I am
overcome by one glance of your eyes,
by a single bead of your necklace.*

SONG OF SOLOMON 4:9 TLB

*My Dear Husband,*

*I love being in your arms. Do you know how wonderful your arms feel
around me? That cozy warmth, that reassuring strength, that stable
security? How perfect it feels when those feelings wrap themselves around
me in the comforting arms of your love. There's something so indescribably
delightful about the physical display of your affection.*

*It's a great way to start a day—or to end it. And, of course, it's
welcome anytime in between. Your embrace reminds me of your constant
love, and it warms my heart with feelings of safety and assurance. So,
wrap your arms around me, my love, and remind me once again that
you're here—that your love is steadfast and dependable. Warm me in your
embrace.*

---

*Dear God, thank You for the capacity to warm and strengthen one
another with something as simple as a hug. Amen.*

# What I Love about You

*The voice of my beloved!*
*Look, he comes, leaping upon the mountains,*
*bounding over the hills.*
*My beloved is like a gazelle or a young stag.*

SONG OF SOLOMON 2:8-9 NRSV

*My Dear Husband,*

*I've so many reasons to love you. Sometimes we get so busy and caught up in the hectic bustle of day-to-day living that, I must confess, I start to take our love for granted. But then, something will make me pause for a moment, and I'll consider all the things I really love about you. Let me try to put some of them into words.*

*I love the way you put others above yourself. And I love the way your heart wants to do what's right. I love the way you treat little children, and animals, and old people. I love the look in your eyes when you're sharing something that's important to you. But best of all, I must admit, I love that you are mine and I am yours.*

---

*Dear God, there are many ways to express our love for one another. But we ask that You would remind us to practice putting our feelings into words. Amen.*

# Separate but One

**Christ himself was like God in everything. But he did not think that being equal with God was something to be used for his own benefit.**

PHILIPPIANS 2:6 NCV

My Dear Husband,

I love the complexities of our relationship. Sometimes the "oneness" of marriage can seem confusing. I know we've been united in love; and yet, without a doubt, we are still two very separate people. We still have very separate views, separate personalities, even separate gifts and abilities. And yet I know that God has made us one. We are one spiritually when we pray together. And we are one physically when we join together in our love for each other. What a great mystery this is.

Despite the ways we are "separate" from each other, God has also created us to become one in His sight. I appreciate the fact that you are so careful to respect my opinions and listen to my point of view. I just want you to know that it means a lot.

---

Dear God, teach us to grow in respect for our differences and yet understand that you see us as one. It's an amazing miracle. Amen.

# Success Is Highly Overrated

*Lay not up for yourselves treasures upon earth, where moth and*
*rust doth corrupt, and where thieves break through and steal:*
*But lay up for yourselves treasures in heaven, where neither*
*moth nor rust doth corrupt, and where thieves*
*do not break through nor steal.*

MATTHEW 6:19-20 KJV

My Dear Husband,

You are my favorite success story. Oh, I know how everyone makes a big deal about "success" these days. But I'm not sure about the way our culture defines that word. I often hear people speak of a "successful life" or of "being successful." But so many times, it seems they are only referring to things like money, prestige, and accumulated wealth.

I'm glad that you are not a man who runs after the world's idea of success—that you would much rather see us living happily and enjoying our relationship. I am so pleased when I see you taking delight in simple everyday pleasures and appreciating the goodness of a life well lived. That, to me, is better than "success." Or perhaps that is the definition of success.

Dear God, thank You for giving us the wisdom to appreciate real success and to recognize the things that really matter. Help us to invest our time and energy in eternal things. Amen.

# What Means Most to Me

*Instead, it should be that of your inner self, the unfading
beauty of a gentle and quiet spirit,
which is of great worth in God's sight.*

1 PETER 3:4 NIV

⋧⋇⋦

*My* Dear Husband,

I love that you care. I love it when I sense you want to do something
really special—something smart and clever, something you think will make
me happy. It's fun to wait for your little surprise to develop. I always enjoy
seeing how you express your affection.

But I have to tell you that what means the most to me is when you take
the time to really listen to what I'm thinking, what I'm concerned about,
what I long for. When you sit down, undisturbed, and look into my eyes
and honestly listen, it means so much. When you ask me how we can
accomplish these things together. When you share your heart. When you take
my hand and whisper that you love me. You are such a blessing to me.

⋧⋇⋦

*Dear* God, the simple things mean so much—thoughtfulness, caring,
and pausing to really listen. Those are the qualities we most appreciate in
You and in each other. Amen.

# True Riches

*Those who want to be rich fall into temptation and are trapped.
... For the love of money is a root of all kinds of evil. ... But as
for you ... pursue righteousness, godliness, faith, love,
endurance, gentleness.*

1 TIMOTHY 6:9-11 NRSV

*My Dear Husband,*

*I bless you for your values. Have you noticed how people seem to be
more and more consumed with the "big bucks?"—making a killing on Wall
Street, winning the lottery, or dreaming of being a guest on the latest
"millionaire" game show? I'm sure it's easy to get caught up in all the
hullabaloo.*

*I want you to know how blessed I feel to have a husband who knows
where true riches lie. I admire the way you are able to keep your eyes on
those things that are real treasures. For earthly riches are only temporary,
and sometimes they bring more problems than they solve. While God's
treasures are truly fulfilling and last forever.*

*Dear God, help us to keep our priorities in order when it comes to
earthly wealth. Show us how to focus our eyes and our energy on You and to
seek out Your imperishable treasures. Amen.*

# What Would I Do Without You?

*Be careful then how you live, not as unwise people but as wise, making the most of the time.*

EPHESIANS 5:15 NRSV

My Dear Husband,

I am so thankful for you. It's not something I like to think about, not something I ever want to experience. But sometimes, just for a flashing moment, I wonder: What would I ever do without you in my life? Where would I be if you were suddenly gone—taken in an instant? And the answer can feel so dismal, so lonely, so sad that I can hardly bare to look.

Of course, I do believe the Lord would sustain me. But I honestly feel that I would be totally lost without you in my life. I think I would be brokenhearted and lonely and—oh, so alone. And because of those feelings, I become more determined than ever to rejoice that you are with me now— to enjoy each and every day that we have together.

---

Dear God, teach us to number our days on earth wisely, knowing that any single one could be our last. Help us to live fully, joyously, lovingly— and without remorse. Amen.

# My Comfort Zone

*Become complete. Be of good comfort, be of one mind,*
*live in peace; and the God of love*
*and peace will be with you.*

2 CORINTHIANS 13:11 NKJV

*My Dear Husband,*

*Being with you puts me at ease. You've heard people say that "everyone needs to step out of their comfort zones from time to time." And while I understand that concept in general, I must protest a little. For you are my comfort zone, my love. And I have no intention of stepping away.*

*I love feeling like I can step into your presence, your arms, your protection, your love—and experience a sense of safety and comfort. And I believe that God gave you to me, specifically, to be my comfort zone. It's just the right place for me. And I hope you feel the same way about me. I hope you can step into my presence and feel at home, loved, safe. I say let's keep our comfort zones.*

---

*Dear God, thank You for giving us the comfort zone of each other's arms. Thank You also for providing a comfort zone for us when we come to You. Amen.*

# Let's Create a Moment

*They will talk together about the glory of your kingdom; they will celebrate examples of your power.*
*They will tell about your mighty deeds and about the majesty and glory of your reign.*

PSALM 145:11-12 NLT

*My Dear Husband,*

*I love those "first times" with you. Remember the first time we met, our first date, the first time you took me into your arms, our first tender kiss? Let's see if we can create another new kind of first together. Let's make some brand new moment—or at least let's do something old in an entirely new and different way. In other words, let's make a fresh memory together.*

*Perhaps we can plan an excursion—a little getaway. How would you feel about getting up early and quietly holding hands as we watch the sun rise over the eastern hills? Maybe we could dream up something totally goofy and unexpected. But whatever it is, let's create something fresh and new—something we both can enjoy and remember in the years to come.*

---

*Dear God, thank You for the gift of spontaneity. Teach us to use it to create new and memorable moments together. Amen.*

# The Way You Walk

*My beloved speaks and says to me: "Arise, my love, my fair one, and come away; for now the winter is past, the rain is over and gone. The flowers appear on the earth; the time of singing has come."*

SONG OF SOLOMON 2:10-12 NRSV

*My Dear Husband,*

*I love seeing you move through life. I can see you coming from a distance, and I know right away that it's you. For you have a certain, unmistakable gait that can only belong to you. And it's just one of those many things about you that I love so much. It's one of those unique qualities that is yours and yours alone. I'm so thankful that God made you just the way He did.*

*And it's the same way with your smile—it's a "one-of-a-kind, light-up-the-room and light-up-my-heart" kind of smile. And there's the way you talk when you're enthused about something or the way that you tell a joke. I love the way you hold your head at a certain angle when you're thinking deeply. All these traits are undeniably you. And how I love them.*

*Dear God, thank You for creating everyone so distinctly different. We appreciate all the unique little things that You have placed in each of us. They are the things that make us who we are. Amen.*

# Our Favorite Song

We praise you, LORD, for all your glorious power.
With music and singing
we celebrate your mighty acts.

PSALM 21:13 NLT

My Dear Husband,

Our love is like sweet music. Doesn't every couple have a special song? Perhaps it's a favorite tune that was popular when they first courted—or a sentimental number performed at their wedding—or even a recent song that holds some special meaning for both of them? What is ours, my love? Do we have one? Let's remember the songs we used to enjoy together; and then let's listen to them again, and let's recall why they were significant back then. Or let's consider what they mean to us now.

And if we can't remember a specific song, then let's put our heads together and come up with one-a brand, new song. And let's make it our own—a milestone for the time we've spent together, a reminder of our romance, a token of our love.

Dear God, music communicates in ways that words fail. Thank You for this wonderful gift that helps us express our love for each other. Amen.

# You're My Soul Mate

*I am overcome with joy because of your unfailing love, for you*
*have seen my troubles, and you care about the anguish of my soul.*
*You have not handed me over to my enemy*
*but have set me in a safe place.*

PSALM 31:7-8 NLT

My Dear Husband,

I love the person deep inside of you. To understand the significance of a soul mate, perhaps we should first consider the substance of the soul—what it is made of. Our souls are the inner part of us that understands the magnificence of creation, that can relish a well-told tale, or revel in a perfect symphony. And we can give thanks to God for giving each of us a unique soul.

And if we're to be soul mates, my love, we need to share some of these soulful pleasures. It can be as simple as admiring a lovely sunset or as complex as understanding an piece of classical literature. But whatever our souls take pleasure in, let's take time to experience these things together.

Dear God, thank You for those things that thrill our souls: music, literature, art, and nature, just to name a few. They enrich our lives and draw us closer together. Amen.

# When I Blow It

*Your heavenly Father will forgive you if you forgive those who
sin against you; but if you refuse to forgive them,
he will not forgive you.*

MATTHEW 6:14-15 TLB

⌒⊚⌒

My Dear Husband,

I bless you for overlooking my faults. Sure, I wish I were perfect, and
I'll admit sometimes I might even act like I am (at least for a moment or
two). But we both know that I'm not. We both know that in reality I'm
human with all the flaws that go with it. And sometimes I just plain blow
it. Whether it's from selfishness, busyness, or just ignorance, the truth is, I
can make some pretty big mistakes.

It makes all the difference in the world, my love, that you are always so
gracious, kind, forgiving, and supportive (okay, almost always). I feel like I
can pick myself up, ask your forgiveness, and go on—and hopefully not
blow it so badly the next time.

⌒⊚⌒

Dear God, help us both to be quick to support the other when we blow
it. Teach us to be gracious and forgiving, as You are. Show us how to lend a
hand to help the other one up. Amen.

# What We're Building

*Unless the LORD builds the house,*
*They labor in vain who build it;*
*Unless the LORD guards the city,*
*The watchman keeps awake in vain.*

PSALM 127:1 NAS

*My Dear Husband,*

*I delight in what we're becoming. Sometimes I lose sight of this thing that we're building together. This thing called love, home, and family. I know how I can get so caught up in the less important details of daily living that I almost forget that you and I are actually constructing something amazingly big—something significant and hopefully something lasting.*

*I want our marriage, our family, our home to be like a city on a high hill—something that people can see from miles around and marvel at. I want our love to shine like a beacon of hope to all who witness it, reminding them that God is good and that grace is real. I want to build something that will continue even after we are gone.*

*Dear God, we need Your help to build this thing. We need Your hands on our lives to make our marriage a monument to You—a symbol of Your love, Your grace, Your mercy, Your forgiveness. Amen.*

# Open Hearts

*Therefore, as God's chosen people, holy and dearly loved, clothe yourselves with compassion, kindness, humility, gentleness and patience. Bear with each other and forgive whatever grievances you may have against one another.*
*Forgive as the Lord forgave you.*

COLOSSIANS 3:12-13 NIV

❦

*My* Dear Husband,

*I love that your heart trusts me. What I long for more than anything in our marriage is to keep my heart open to you—and for you to do the same with me. But I know it's not easy to remain in this position of vulnerability—at least not continuously. Misunderstandings come and hurts happen; and before I know it, our hearts are closing up again.*

*But forgiveness and love can open a heart's closed door. And as we learn to trust each other more completely, we can reassure one another that our love is a safe place, a secure haven. And that's when our hearts open up, and we begin to share deeply.*

❦

*Dear God, help us to create a relationship that's safe and secure and trustworthy. Teach us to keep our hearts open so that our love can mature and grow. Amen.*

# I Remember When . . .

*I remember what the LORD did;*
*I remember the miracles you did long ago.*
*I think about all the things you did*
*and consider your deeds.*

PSALM 77:11-12 NCV

**M**y Dear Husband,

*I bless you for those wonderful yesterdays. I remember the first time our eyes met in a look that said, "There's something going on here." I remember the rush that ran through me—the electricity in the air. I remember the first time you wrapped your hand around mine, the warmth, the security. I remember thinking I'll always be safe in your arms.*

*I remember the first time you wiped away my tears, holding me close and comforting me with your blanket of love. We have shared and gone through so much together—so many experiences, so many memories. Let's take time to remember these things together—to celebrate them once more.*

*D*ear God, what a long way we've come. When we think of all we've gone through, the places we've been—both the rewarding and the trying—we're so thankful that we've had Your help and support all along the way. Amen.*

# Planning Romance

*I decided it was more important to enjoy life. The best that people can do here on earth is to eat, drink, and enjoy life, because these joys will help them do the hard work God gives them here on earth.*

ECCLESIASTES 8:15 NCV

My Dear Husband,

*I love it when you make intimate plans. When we were young and freshly in love, it seemed that romance just happened. We didn't seem to go to a lot of trouble; just being together was enough. But we did make plans to be together—didn't we? I can remember sometimes it was all I could think about—you and me, together, walking, talking, laughing, sharing.*

*But times have changed, and life's a lot busier these days. And now it makes sense to plan for romance. I recognize the need to take time to schedule a date and make preparations for a feeling of romantic ambiance. And just because these moments don't "just happen" doesn't mean they're any less meaningful. In fact, like a well-choreographed ballet, they can be delightful.*

---

Dear God, *teach us new ways to bring creativity and imagination into our love. Amen.*

# Our Sweet Secrets

*How sweet is your love, my darling, my bride. How much better it is than mere wine. The perfume of your love is more fragrant than all the richest spices.*

SONG OF SOLOMON 4:10 TLB

My Dear Husband,

I love our private times together. I love knowing that I can trust you with my most intimate secrets, and that these things will remain private—just a sweet confidence shared between the two of us. This level of trust is one of my favorite things about married life. Having someone I can safely trust and confide in is a precious gift. I love knowing you won't betray me or let me down.

And I want you to know your secrets are just as safe with me. I want you to be secure in my ability to maintain a confidence. For we need to protect those private places in our relationship, places where no one else can enter. And we need to put our heads together and whisper without fear of being overheard. And then our trust will flourish and grow.

Dear God, teach us each day to develop listening ears, understanding hearts, and the ability to keep a confidence. Amen.

# Let's Talk about Eternity

*Love never fails. But where there are prophecies, they will cease;*
*where there are tongues, they will be stilled; where there is*
*knowledge, it will pass away.*

1 CORINTHIANS 13:8 NIV

·◈·

*M*y Dear Husband,

*I want our love to go on and on. We have promised that our love will*
*live forever—or at least "until death do us part." But I realize our*
*earthbound minds don't understand the concept of forever all that well.*
*Only God can comprehend such things. And sometimes I wonder what it*
*will be like in the hereafter. What will become of our love?*

*And that's when I realize, all I can do is trust God—believing that*
*He's the One who has bound our hearts together, and only He knows what*
*will happen to our relationship in light of eternity. But this one thing I*
*know, I believe in my heart our love will continue. In some shape or form,*
*I feel certain it will go on. Because real love cannot die.*

·◈·

*D*ear God, some things are too great for our human, finite minds to
*understand—things like, what happens to our relationship when there's no*
*such thing as marriage in Heaven. But we know we can trust You with these*
*questions. And like little children, we know You know best. Amen*

# Our Love Complete

**Being confident of this, that he who began a good work in you will carry it on to completion until the day of Christ Jesus.**

PHILIPPIANS 1:6 NIV

*My* Dear Husband,

*I delight how our love grows stronger. Even if I attempted to love you with everything within me, I realize even that would not be a complete and perfect love. For I am only human and cannot help but make mistakes. My love, though sincere, can often fall short—missing the mark or stopping too soon. But I believe God can complete my love. He can enable me to go the extra step and love you selflessly and with my whole heart.*

*I want to learn to let God love through me like this. I want to become all that I can be in our marriage-to be kinder, more loving, more generous in our relationship. But I know it will take time, commitment, and, most of all, God, to make my love for you complete.*

*Dear God, You've begun a good work in our marriage; You've planted your seeds of love in our hearts. But we realize that only You can bring our love to a place of completion. And we know it's a lifelong process. We pray that You'll help us to cooperate with Your plan. Amen.*

# A Shared Vision

**Patient endurance is what you need now,
so you will continue to do God's will.
Then you will receive all that he has promised.**

HEBREWS 10:36 NLT

◦◦◦◦

My Dear Husband,

I love it when we're spiritually united,. As our love and relationship grow, I hope we can begin to share a vision for what our Father God would have us do together. For I believe He united us for a special reason, something beyond our own personal fulfillment and delight (although we enjoy those things too!). And I look forward to serving God, side by side, in some unique way.

I long to see God utilize our relationship to touch others. I desire that our marriage might become an outreach of love and kindness to those around us. For when our cup is so full, how can we hold back the richness of blessings? How can we keep all God's grace and goodness to ourselves? For I know, as we share, we shall also receive.

◦◦◦◦

Dear God, we pray You'll give us a clear vision of what You'd like to do in our lives. Show us ways You can bless others through our relationship. Pour Yourself through us and onto others. Amen.

# Together Forever

*Surely goodness and mercy shall follow me*
*All the days of my life;*
*And I will dwell in the house of the LORD Forever.*

PSALM 23:6 NKJV

*My Dear Husband,*

*I love you forever and ever. Although we don't fully understand the complexities of what our relationship will be when we step into the grandeur and majesty of our heavenly home, I do believe we'll be there together. I do believe that you, my husband, my closest earthly friend, will still be by my side, holding my hand in yours. I want us to be together forever.*

*I want to stand by your side as we gaze in wide-eyed wonder upon those heavenly gates. I want to walk with you as we travel those glimmering streets of gold. I want to bow down, next to you, as we worship the King of all kings. And I firmly believe that our union will remain as strong—yes, even stronger—than it is here on earth.*

*Dear God, thank You for bringing us together for this earthly pilgrimage called life. We look forward to spending eternity getting to know You better. Amen.*